the *she said* dialogues:
flesh memory

the *she said* dialogues:
flesh memory

akilah oliver

Nightboat Books
New York

ISBN: 978-1-64362-034-3

Cover art by Barbieo Barros Gizzi, "The She Said Dialogues," 1999
Used with permission of the artist
Author photo by Teresa Hurst
Design and typesetting by HR Hegnauer
Text set in Sabon

the she said dialogues: flesh memory was originally published by Smokeproof
Press/Erudite Fangs Editions in 1999.

Earlier versions of these poems have appeared in *Bombay Gin*; *Spike::4*; *High
Risk 2: Writings on Sex, Death, and Subversion*; *Fast Talk, Full Volume:
An Anthology of Contemporary African American Betry*; and *The Little
Magazine, Volume 19*.

Many thanks to the colleagues and friends whose graciousness made this book
possible: Michelle T. Clinton for being there during the early years; Heather
Riley for her magic; Cynthia Davis for her love; Brad O'Sullivan for the
endless hours given without complaint; and of course, Anne Waldman for her
unwavering vision and generosity of spirit.

Cataloging-in-publication data is available from the Library of Congress

Nightboat Books
New York
www.nightboat.org

Contents

Akilah's Sentry, Spatial Truth

I find myself searching for her. Still. In the echo of what *she said*. I cannot ask her any questions. This introduction is a stop-and-start reverberation. I miss her, I stop. I miss her and start. This open space, the page, opens wounds and memories. Insights, incisions, parted lips.

This is not a eulogy, this is, as they say in jazz, "sitting in." The poems dialogue, take me, back. In reading this collection one cannot help but fall into perspectival shifts in locus, in moments. From halcyon notions of Africa in the hearts of African-Americans, ideas that crack under the pressure of racist reality, to the space-time rifts that create flashes of real freedom in the fullness of lesbian sexuality. Akilah's precise, innovative, extraordinary work takes us to revealed places in the body, places where life has failed us and yet new beginnings may be possible. Her debut collection seems to call to us, saying: we have this kind of gathering together, a collective state of being called *she* and this state can advise us, speak to us, it is whom we can trust with our secrets, fears, hopes and setbacks.

Often this work reminds me of what it was like to grow up a young Black woman in the 1990s, the hope of Black power, like mother's milk in our childhoods, crushed under the weight of the relentless state as well as betrayed by its own contradictions. What we experienced still inhabits the body and mind; it sneaks around back to us, like an unexpected death. It's fitting that this book is replete with unfulfilled wishes for the world we hope for.

The text of this book is stunning in its clear-eyed consideration of desire and regret. Throughout the volume I am struck by how often the speaker, who is talking to *she* or reflecting on the advice of *she*, speaks to the truth that there is no perfect place for Black people, Black women, Black activists, Black lesbians, Black queer folk:

> *what was i supposed to say*
> that i loved you is too simple a lie. when i breathe your face
> & see i am stunned with sight of you warrior girl your
> wounds i want to cry in & suck blood. everything pales in
> comparison. this is the secret of power. corruption so easy.
> i want to sing a revolutionary song. dress in fatigue. kick
> ass. lick pussy. did you say you are not black. you are not
> white. create a theoretical language to situate the emotion.
> i admit none of this. the exhibitionist just likes to expose
> her scars.
> —from "summon, she said, her by the name you loved"

However, there can be perfect *moments* in communing with the (deified) *she*, as well as moments of exalted self-acceptance in sharing the body's desire with another woman, this particular closeness, a sometimes spiritual and definitively physical communion. This is the opposite of forgetting oneself; all the baggage of the regular world is brought in, yet love is there anyway. In this work, sometimes these women are Black, sometimes they are not, but the Blackness of the speaking woman is at the core of each intimacy. Every poem is always truthful, and the body is the fullness of truth:

> go back to start. look surprised at the trickery. again. such
> faith keeps me going. god loves us don't you know child.
> comfort. i could have sworn it was her on the street. it was
> her on my page. it was her true form stretched across my
> bed. her left breast on my lip. nipple reddish brown.
> galaxies skipping over my stretch marks. dreams. they got
> me. how are you.
> —from "is you is or is you ain't"

As a queer, Black, innovative, intellectual woman, mother of her son Oluchi, daughter, sister, performer and spell-casting poet, Akilah poured all, and different aspects, of herself into these pages: sometimes as her vulnerable, flawed self; sometimes as the perfected deified other, or, one could say, the superego. Akilah's grounded and varying positions, her performance of herself in these different voicings, are just a few of the considerations that perfume the book. Akilah, smartly, doesn't seek to make peace between these aspects, to make them work together, she simply acknowledges that they exist for her, confront her, sometimes soothe her, simultaneously. They coexist. Short declarative lines potently cycle throughout this work. Keeping the sentences clipped and ending in periods, it's as if the lines accept each other in the same point in time, irrespective of when and where they occur. There is a tension between the period and the word that follows, usually without capitalization to underscore the non-hierarchy of letters, words, phrases, experiences, moments and punctuation. By using the blocked stanza form, Akilah seems to underscore that there is no beginning or end. Everything *is*, whether past, present or future; events can even be superimposed with current consciousness:

you a visitor in a landscape you don't control.

i want to know what the eyes smelled at the bottom of the ships. i've seen that look of terror before. any asshole on the bus pants hanging off his butt. X terrorizing a fashion statement on hats & tee shirts. any black boy beautiful or ugly could be of my blood. one meaning of blackness. this arbitrariness of circumstance. know it's all possible & nothing's true.
   where's the national museum with the slave ships. whips. neck silencers. irons. chains. mouth bits. if i said
      the ships.
why wouldn't we all immediately have a common reference.

—from "she said loss, lost"

The past is her tapestry, a brocade in a poetry room, where ornate melodies are also played in various keys. The same song, same *feel,* may come around again differently if you are still and wait to hear it. About halfway through the book, Akilah asks, through a poem title, "so where do you enter memory?" and *she* is not (necessarily) asking the question. This interlude is a pause for the speaker to orient us to the expansive thinking that develops as the book progresses. It also raises the question of *how* one enters memory. Akilah uses many devices in assessing where and how. This poem's title is also one of the few in the book that doesn't have the word *she* in it. Yet *she* is ever-present in memory and the moment, and the all-knowing, rueful, *she* is sorely needed. The *she* dialoguing (the "shes," really) can be understood as our best, most knowing selves. The "us" here is womanist, queer and Afrocentric and makes room for other women too, other Black people, integrationists, revolutionaries, everyone in the world. However, *she* is the immovable spirit, the first ancestor in this matrifocality, grounded in a particular tradition and perspective as Akilah makes clear in her preface. It is the memory of a particular type of flesh:

> ...the dialogues seek to work as a kind of insurgent text within the African American literary tradition. I see the dialogues as part of the emerging outsider tradition in black literature which restates memory and identity in a post-Civil Rights framework. A framework which is multiplicitous. Which supports a dialogue that questions and challenges existentialist notions of what an African American literary dialogue does/ can be. Stretching the dialogue. Admitting the contractions. Investigating the truths.

Lush images, striking framing and embedded multiplicities of place, time and point of view generate language that doesn't feel staccato despite the end-stops (e.g.: "rain streaks blood down river. gushing teenagers in love / carpool thru. your eyes go away from me. simple pleasures. / breasts to breasts."—from "lover, she says, dare you hold my sorrow"). We negotiate the intensity between those (menstrual) periods, and yes, that pun is very much in the work. There is a steady beat that those stops provide us. As we read the cycle, a kind of incantatory quality begins to synch our heartbeats, our blood with hers.

> so this is what you ancients meant by crying time. i have
> not been good. i have not been bad. sometimes i haven't
> been nothing at all. grey haired lady. white haired lady.
> perfect witch of high pitch. bathe me nice in kitchen sink.
>   —from "she said, talk to grandmother in cycles"

Here, Akilah refashions the idea of baptism and makes it hex-magical and women-centered, "beautiful and faithful and ancient / and female and brave" (to draw from Lucille Clifton's "poem in praise of menstruation"). Here the bravery comes from telling the truth, confessing to older women you can tell the "real deal" to, who may advise you but who raised, or leveled, you with the salvation to cleanse wounds.

The rhythm of incantation extends to Black music. Akilah explicitly references Curtis Mayfield here, as a radioed voice, in ether, like Tina Turner's, filling the body yet disembodied: *"What's love got to do, got to do with it. I learned to say / boombox"* (from "The Absence of the Lover Makes Her Who She Is"). Akilah, in stretching the usual discourse around African-American culture, reframes Black music, questioning aspects of it that the status quo accepts. Akilah is showing us the world as it is for queer Black women, and complacent, non-inquisitive Muzak is also subject to inspection through an opposition to banality: "a secret uncommercialized in advertisements. / & the taste of a porch sunken in north st. louis / leaves your lips blackened" (from "pick any curtis mayfield song to accompany this").

The Black woman's ever-blackening body and its flexibility (lowering, leveling, raising, stretching) is related to "galaxies skipping over my stretch marks. dreams." (from "is you is or is you ain't"). These references come across not only as stretch but also as "tautness." Her *lines* are tight, a mirror of that embodied extension. Saying this phrase to *she,* without being judged by her, is an understanding of the body as liaison, aspecting the speaker's changing states.

> we try not to drown & close
> to floating is the saddest kind of survival
> —from "another morning, she says"

We start this poem with a whole sea, which the Bible reminds us can be magically parted, and yet we end with not fully living but surviving only. All the heightened images, the sharp perceptions that are contained between those two couplets do not ultimately matter because *we are just trying to make it out here in these streets*, she seems to often say in this collection. This first poem introduces us to the totality of the world within the book.

Fittingly, the last poem in the collection and one of the longest, "Lover: II," reminds us of her start. The first enjambed line is:

> no not that part.   the part that made sense. like when your mother
> called you
> The Tramp.

The last line of the poem and the cycle is:

> *yes, when I was five.*

The italicization is an underscore and important to note here. Who is the first love, therefore the first disappointment? She was a *she* too. There is an unmistakable reference to Freud here, psychoanalysis being just one facet of Akilah's elegant theoretical moves throughout this book.

The premise of the title of *the she said dialogues* and the poems within it preclude the assumption of performance and its subjectivity. In one of our last conversations, Akilah and I gushed over Judith Butler, Butler's interest and study of the philosopher J.L. Austin's notion of the performative and Butler's seismic-shifting assertion of the subjectivity of gender and the constructions of the idea through language. Long before her formal study of Butler, Akilah, in *the she said dialogues*, investigates the generating of gender notions as *she* in this book. As the epigraph to my foreword shows, Akilah continued to cultivate her poetics beyond this debut book, *in conversation with others* and the othered, as well as aspects of herself, on multiple realms.

From the vantage point of the reader there is the listener/advisee and *she*, the speaker and advisor. *she* is a poet, *she is poetry*. Poetry is exalted as a queer, Black womanist uttering being. Akilah brings us into this majesty of personified womanness, uncompromised and attuned. The receivers (the relaying speaker and us, as readers) are all performing this discourse with *she* together: as confession, inquiry and wish-fulfillment.

There are multiple levels at which this book encourages listening. What's stunning about the collection, in 1999 and today, is that Akilah preemptively expands her audience of listeners. Those of us who approach language in non-conformist ways, especially those who are multiply marginalized, feel welcomed in this collection with our whole selves. Those who are more accustomed to convention appreciate how her craft makes them feel. Those who are not in niche poetry communities, the *people*, are welcomed here. These poems, individually and together, present easeful technical mastery and the soul of the writer. Her private, rigorous exploration is *with* us and with *she*. Innovative poets come from people, they come from *peeps,* those audible flitterings, punctuated sounds, where the truth of the heart lives. While flush with philosophy and technique, these poems shape themselves for her people, from her family to the people at the bar, the young folks from "around the way," the revolutionaries and the language innovators from the church pews to the ivory tower.

On the cover is an unblinking eye, a sentry at the end of the century. One dreadlock is its curtain, its whip. A coiled, looped drawstring, unending, unnoosed, untied. The eye is not just unwavering, it *can't* close. It's so *close*. The frame cuts the image. The cyclops, her all-seeing eye, that singular *lock* of hair is where the metaphysical meets the physical. The *she* engages with the body and the body with *she*, their veracity for all to see.

> symmetrical truths. the nonsense takes all night. a way to
> survive the dark. peer at first light. the choir in robes
> crimson.
> menstrual blood of angels. i bleed.
> > —from "gently she tucks her hand under my chin, she says,
> > don't be afraid, your demons are your friends"

and

i supposed to say
the physical suck is never enough. moons have coalesced
to confuse the day. take a slow train home. this is the long
way. dissent. ahhh breath & feel better you radicals of steel.
draw lines around the stomach that has birthed stretch
marks. reject the smooth playboy image of femininity. lick.
                —from "summon, she said, her by the name you loved"

In "refashioning the Black female tongue" (from the last sentence of
her preface), Akilah is doing the opposite of tongue-*twisting*. She's
loosening. Yet more than reportage, she foments disturbed seas in us, the
readers. What do we make of all this? The book's metanarrative is that
she advises us on how to manage ourselves in this world:

another morning, she says
first take before sunrise, she said
gently she tucks her hand under my chin, she says,
        don't be afraid, your demons are your friends
sin and salvation are twins
once upon a time, she said
think of the words as angels singing in your vagina, she said
handing me the needle, she said here, make your wish
several paths to yourself, she said
it doesn't matter how you fall into light, she said
i think, she said, you'd be happier if you could remember
        a wise saying
sickness can be salvation, she said
so, she said, this is what we've been missing
we forget, she said
she said, let the little squeals assemble
well why wouldn't you, she said
she said loss, lost
it's just a mental journey
cross the great divide, she said
she is more than useful fiction
summon, she said, her by the name you loved
pick any curtis mayfield song to accompany this

she said, talk to grandmother in cycles
she said,
is you is or is you ain't
under the bedspread, those smells, maybe nobody will notice
so where do you enter memory
lover, she says, dare you hold my sorrow
she says
saturday, she says
she said, meditate on rage
speak in the two voices
tell me a story, she says
come to me when you can't speak she said
she said, again
the grass is always greener, she said
she said, own it
she said, don't give up
tressles of hair, she said
she said, talk to grandmother in cycles: cycle 3
she said, sometimes love's rage will just eat you alive, won't it?
cross the line, she said
she said, treasure it
she said, heather
The Absence of the Lover Makes Her Who She Is
Lover: I
Lover: II

This list of poem titles from the book is one poem, and explicates the relationship between the speaker and *she*. They present the wisdom of *she,* her truth, compassion and care. *She* wants the speaker and we, as readers, to *live*, to thrive in unflinching truth including what the body in its desire knows. *She* is "true north" and if that means seeing that all hell is breaking loose and is "going south" so be it. So *she* it. Two women souls are speaking to each other. This is the nature of their discourse. The definite article of the collection's title serves to prepare us for the firmness of the speaking even if what is being noted is difficult to bear.

While there is so much engagement with the body in this collection, Akilah leaves us with the ethereal *place* of the dialogue with *she*. The body is only one part of the self. It defines us some, but we can change those definitions, just as we can free ourselves from the expectations the outside world has for *how* our bodies are allowed to exist in it, even if we defy those conventions for just a moment. This defiance can be with the sexual body of another, or there might be another moment of defiance (or the same moment) when we are merged with our highest selves. *the she said dialogues: flesh memory* are poems that touch us through the body, through the mind, through our spirits, through our indomitable ancestry and flesh that lives in *she*, the everlasting spirit. Akilah makes plain the constraints of real time, and yet there is friction, and potentially freedom within these lines.

—Tracie Morris
Brooklyn, NY

About the poems

The American Heritage College Dictionary Definitions:

flesh (flesh) *n.* 1.a. the soft tissue of the body of a vertebrate, consisting mainly of skeletal muscle and fat. b. the surface or skin of the human body. 2. the meat of animals as distinguished from the edible tissue of fish or fowl. 3. Bot. the pulpy, usu. edible part of a fruit or a vegetable. 4. excess fatty tissue; plumpness. 5.a. the body as opposed to the mind or soul. b. the physical or carnal nature of humanity. c. sensual appetites. 6. humankind in general; humanity. 7. one's family; kin. 8. substance; reality. [ME<Œ *flœsc.*)

memory (mem' e re) 1. the mental faculty of retaining and recalling past experience. 2. the act or instance of remembering; recollection. 3. all that a person can remember. 4. something remembered. 5. the fact of being remembered; remembrance: *dedicated to their memory.* 6. the period of time covered by remembrance or recollection of a person or group of persons. [ME *memorie*<AN<Lat. *memoria, memor*, mindful]

Post-Modern Poetry & Performance Art Definition:

flesh memory (flesh mem' e re) 1. a text, a language, a mythology, a truth, a reality, an invented as well as literal translation of everything that we've ever experienced or known, whether we know it directly or through some type of genetic memory, osmosis or environment. 2. the body's truths and realities. 3. the multiplicity of languages and realities that the flesh holds. 4. the language activated in the body's memory.

What I am trying to do in these poems is investigate the non-linear synapses between desire, memory, blackness (as both a personal identity and a non-essentialist historical notion), sexuality and language. There are many encoded references to pop culture, gospel music and African American colloquial speech. The block form is a kind of container to hold the 'narrative' or dialogue for some of the pieces. I see the poems very much as an exploration of 'flesh memory,' as a field of investigation. I think for me part of the importance of this text is situated in the on-going work I've been doing in performance with the concept of flesh memory as it relates to a critical interrogation of the African American literary/performative tradition. That tradition (what I consider to be crouched in the sacred/profane dichotomy, a dichotomy which DuBois called 'double consciousness') is an out-growth of a necessitated survival mechanism, which has split 'Black consciousness,' not only in terms of the outward, homogenous mask donned as a form of cultural preservation, but also in terms of the internal discourse: what is permissible to speak.

The work I've been doing consciously seeks to disrupt this tradition, to play not only with language and form, but with the representational idioms of 'blackness,' 'femaleness,' 'homogeneity.' The bluntness of the sexual references (often linking the sacred traditions [church gospel/ icons] with the profane [pussy/fucking]) is one way the dialogues seek to work as a kind of insurgent text within the African American literary tradition. I see the dialogues as part of the emerging outsider tradition in black literature which restates memory and identity in a post-Civil Rights framework. A framework which is multiplicitous. Which supports a dialogue that questions and challenges existentialist notions of what an African American literary dialogue does/can be. Stretching the dialogue. Admitting the contractions. Investigating the truths. Making itself up as it goes. Refashioning the Black female tongue.

—Akilah Oliver
November 1998

the *she said* dialogues:
flesh memory

another morning, she says

a red sea of ambrosia is my god's nectar
& my god's anonymity wails in tongues
pawned in once a negro time to st. louis a little girl
with grandma & cold fried chicken did go &
passenger trains shank underground & desire & need
sweat under armpits & i smell streets
& sad morning rises like baptismal mist
from the steamy holy water in which
we try not to drown & close
to floating is the saddest kind of survival

first take before sunrise, she said

sweet tongue sifting stained glass over dust tracks down a
road that ain't georgia.
this time of dark morning. this is the face i give for
scarification.
unbathed.
this is the teeth i use in plural disagreement. a people
long ways from shore.
this is the ear. no. these is the ears. i want to hear sound
slight as gesture.
bellowing way down in my belly.
baby.
way down in my belly. bellowing way down.
disquieting morning i breathe. an act outside my will.
strangely lifelike.

gently she tucks her hand under my chin, she says, don't be afraid, your demons are your friends

night becomes you so said little angels dressed in red on the way home from parties where the dead bless the damned. confusions date the air. smoke goes easily into passageways between dreams & regret. passed onto those who will themselves generations. rams with aries tags skittering across wide boulevards in brownie uniforms. think the pledge worthy of remembrance. how do you wake the dead cushioned in sheepskin car seat covers. enter the angel. some hair lingers in her armpits. pick up the butts to smoke. down in the street they lay in shades of blackness. not the celebrated dreams of nationalist visionaries who want it all romantic or nothing. look for lit veils. there are so many ways to pass the time on earth. the sorrow the grief stands in line to be recognized.

stop to hold me.

sidewalk voices cry out. grocery baskets with debris of lives stacked high. you have to pray at the mission before you get food. you have to pretend jesus loves you. have to pretend you care.

all the things i want are in mountains & oceans & flowers delicate as baby's blood. my blood. bury the placenta & come home. breasts echo. promise & good times & chopped wood.

travel down a road. a horizon. wolves mark desert night. slow dance at house parties. reality unarmed. everybody have a good time. alright you freaks. stereo. red black green beads dangle from afrofashion braids. who betrayed the dream.. flimsy protection of skin. sheds its collective memory time & time again. they are all so innocent with their pimples on.

snort the perfume.

feel better now. on the way to somewhere the little child said it's such a nice town. they must be hiding something. pleasantries & manners & southern california slave culture. snip. the girls took sewing the boys took shop & the worlds were ordered reams of notebook paper. then your mama slaps you in the face. then you vomit in an alley in a strange town. then you fuck yourself with a cucumber dildo. then you feel good. then you look at all the gun toting boys in ice cube scowls calling you bitch & you disengage. then you put some dope in the pipe. & you smoke it & you feel nothing. then the sun cuts clouds razor edged & redemptive. & you feel, sigh. evil over arid city hustles food.

stop the progression of civilization. the pursuit of happiness is killing. as seen through partially opened blinds. telephone wires stretch across sky. tops of trees. christian cross in clouds.

symmetrical truths. the nonsense takes all night. a way to survive the dark. peer at first light. the choir in robes crimson.
menstrual blood of angels. i bleed.

red.
patron color of grief.
& birth.
& all forms of self inflicted wounds.

sin and salvation are twins

summer lets go its sail. touches the bottom of my gut. the
soul does similar tricks without an audience. i see. i see there
is no separation between the earth & sky. elvis presley
already died to be anointed king by ghost seekers.
compartments of space invented to live in. artificial
dominions of good & evil fail to impress. the great depths
to which i am likely to fall. search for soul. i don't mind if
jesus is my friend. i want my friends to answer when i call.
faces of children smeared with lullabies to a redundant
satan. it is not that i am personally guilty. only culpable.
capable of falling. more probable than flying.

once upon a time, she said

old folks. scotch & malt liquor in da living room. do the mash potato child. break it up. upholstery plasticized. uncle spooky tales sandwiched between floorboards. justify the continuation. lives go on & on. so free of godly instincts. open those doors & let me breathe. no sea takes me home. i witness bones on the atlantic floor. chiseled faces. short vowel sounds trapped under centuries of sediment. let the cow jump over the moon. tell momma you love her. don't think you can live no more in that room. all the exquisite summertime. gone. mash potato. child.

think of the words as angels singing in your vagina, she said

i'm a mentally well schizophrenic. i fuck ghosts i know by name. 1975.
radio says I want this pain to stop.   bedspread friction. chorus.   for a long time afterwards the rush is enough. see isn't that nice. oh stretch marks i want to make you a shrine of doll heads & penes. nibble on a metaphor. i say when i am unable to say anything. but then you had to go. a long time afterwards bloodstains on your tee-shirt were smashed rose petals. the stains. innocence.

rain is it you waking me in slumber or is that my lovers' voices crashed against smooth black.

continuous orgasm. bites pavement. glass popping. bristly hairs rub lavender. my tongue swallows whole all the seductions. wet. taste me. i could have been at home between your legs. how she sing like that. how she sing like that. how she know just then is when i need to cry. it's the reciprocity of beauty that makes me doubt my self. you. it's the wetness i want. a vessel into the endless zone where no roles exist. amen. understand the blood comes out like this. jagged sky. if you don't believe me no verbs will follow the suicides noun.

don't just stand there.
thank them for coming.

handing me the needle, she said here,
make your wish

simple language of a tree.
i misunderstood.   so used to the shouts of lips.
sit up & tie your shoelaces.
mute with a stolen voice.
the well slept dream always has a twist.
white patent leather shoes dangling from a chair.
why take these little things to heart.
dear somebody.   cover my tracks.
i cannot feel myself. my bones are not mine.
orphan sky adopt me please. humanity has not been kind.
applaud. faces etched in glass. crude animals pose.
your mama's good looking.
words fly.
capable of decapitation. what i would want.

several paths to yourself, she said

in front of k-mart a man collects coins for a pan-african jesus. white & slow flakes collect a cascading love in my hair. simple acts. cars pass through. who can tell love in these times when children break like expendable dolls in hands of those who will later plead a biological defense. they are extensions of my anger. he cried too much. she wanted too much. situate in the moment. beer foam melts into glass. who will remember the way it was. safe. when knowledge was knowing words of a commercial ditty. dance to extinction. i want to be a rock-n-roll star. i want my excesses congratulated. in a movie once. in a school once. the tenement dwelling boy saved a cat. his welfare mother in house coat when he got home. i liked the idea of a strong mother until i was one. a tenderness in poverty. face it. you another statistic. thinking these words will make you special. someone said we were the first generation to reap the benefits of desegregation. black kids in compton call mexicans white. nonono i cry. the white people are all dancing on soul train. how strange this privilege. the telling of the story may be more important than the story itself. those who loved without condition wear placards on their breasts. brush a shriveled finger across your speaking lips. ask if you've misplaced your name.

it doesn't matter how you fall into light, she said

now approach holiness in memory.
wizard scatters leaves. the little things. basking out the
window.   air adorned aches.
to be invented. vulgarize the living sentence. trampled
daisies.
a mind. shake the long night. unplanted placenta. every
failed insurrection in cotton fields. i am where the sun has
gone. sugarcane and pathetic.
look ma. no hands.
bodies jump overboard. taste is addiction enough. when
horny think of sexuality & gods. less than 100 identified in
l.a. county. a bell tinkles on a ice cream truck. i shouldn't
be no ways tired. tell me it's saturday. reason to wear
something new. it's all right. breathe their air. the urge to
kiss. all this time i thought i should have done something
else.

i think, she said, you'd be happier
if you could remember a wise saying

home. repeat like prayer. winter is here. see the torn brick.
soured breakfast juice. seems like a good description. folks
won't ask no questions. see it all fits together.
find another rainbow.

all the music.
otis redding singing in algeria.   damn.
an exclamation.   i added.   the world of machines
a necessary imposter. i guess the P
stands for panther. i don't claim all of the action.
only the dream.

sickness can be salvation, she said

night angels sent me wailing across mine fields.
wake up. do you want to rock-n-roll. i could have said stop.
i wanted to see it enter. come on & have a ball.
how far the sky goes.
nobody be careful then act infinite.
i say the soul.
i say my soul. inaccessible to whims.
done with linear thoughts. pele on heroin twisting behind
chicken wire. stutter. clouds bellow in spanish. i could have
said stop. i wanted to see the needle enter. who would have
thought we'd mourn. innocent wonder of it all. i wish i could
speak without betraying somebody's delusions.
willful confusion.
as if we could be contained in a given time. pass the sugar.
the honey's all crystallized.

so, she said, this is what we've been missing

golden valleys all of us tumbling thru. a wayward grasp at
flying. such scenery we are we like to view.
go head on.
snap snap snap.
walk away from the center of reality. i don't know where
that is at. forget what is said in the world of touch. anything
you want baby. marilyn monroe promised. ride flames
thrashing thighs. find a field where plantain & cucumber
grow. eat from the vulva's sphere. snapshots endure. smile
lucky. the world is a firecracker &
don't you forget it.
you safe.
all those kids missing on milk cartons. fall away from the
centerfold. small breasts alone on a beach.
sing.
this is imperative. all this time away from heaven.
all this.

we forget, she said

i want the metaphor clear.
i want to clarify. you get what you want if you want it hard
enough. bullshit. take it like truth. gurus & gods. tender
buttons. i wanted to say that. weight. if we wasn't at least
half spirit why do we always be trying to fly. angels in
distress. jamborees in the morning. slick taste of cocaine
chorusing down throats. i never saw a clown i liked.
subterranean train stations. gum & cigarettes & strange
candy wrappers. men. eyeing the foreigner. me. all the time
i hear pieces of st. louis. somewhere in the clouds. carly
simon. clouds in my coffee. a pop reference. why pretend
we hear plato speak. open wide. send the soldiers out to
pasture. ice t. snickers his high yellow niggah badder than
the best don't fuck with me stance. champions we be. waves
recede. how come we don't make anymore mythology. in
finland once all night the sky was day.

she said, let the little squeals assemble

talk around the obvious. the whole country's going to shit. &
you too. & me. a street.   stuffed with flowers.
warehouses of scents. dog doo on the path.
a man cries dry coughs.
let's go for a field trip kiddies. up up & away. the cow.
was it the cow.   was it a moon.   prostitute.
caught up in a groove.
repeat offenders.   jump.   yeah.   keep time.
papa don't take no stuff. jealous breasts around the maypole. hunt the
illusion down. faraway languages sound check the air.   right.
i want my pen to flourish. fancy deaths.
off shoulder strapless black.   cliche.
linger unknowingly in lit spaces. fire beckons.
always call first. like a good girl. pretend to be deaf.

well why wouldn't you, she said

discard the proud robe of victim. sky is whistling. oh the
little earthlings. some other synonym for free. move. the
beat of another drummer. shhhh. we're having a brilliant
time.
sexual acts performed in the town square. town mall. woo
the angels. only a woman can empty so fully. the beauty
that is the pain's opposite. honey. inhale their air. cover my
eyes. silly bandit. this is the way i want you to kiss me.

she said loss, lost

tina turner on acid yodeling in arabic.
however goes the night.
yesterday rocks touched my feet. seaweed soaked jeans in
pigeon stained sand. pigeons masquerading as seagulls.
haven't seen them for a long time. lots of things gone. bell
on an ice cream truck. my favorite line already happened.
on the radio a voice sounds like a teasing three year old &
the horn section goes nanananana. all cocky. closed fisted
salutes. how come nobody mentioned clitorectomy with
they dashikis on. like we were afraid a close look. a
criticism. a rejection of a fixed ritual would pop the bubble.
dreams are fragile like that. concealing as much as they
reveal. colors proscribed in song. imagining the world as
placed.   fixed.

you a visitor in a landscape you don't control.

i want to know what the eyes smelled at the bottom of the
ships. i've seen that look of terror before. any asshole on
the bus pants hanging off his butt. X terrorizing a fashion
statement on hats & tee shirts. any black boy beautiful or
ugly could be of my blood. one meaning of blackness. this
arbitrariness of circumstance. know it's all possible &
nothing's true.
    *where's the national museum with the slave ships. whips.
neck silencers. irons. chains. mouth bits. if i said*
        the ships.
why wouldn't we all immediately have a common reference.
where is the national tongue. the informed language for
this thing called slavery. i don't know of anyone who knows

the names of their great great great great grandfathers. not the mythic ones or adopted ones. the exact people who birthed you. i don't know of anyone who knows the faces of their grandmothers' rapists. not any face. the face. i don't know anyone who can sing an old freedom song. where are the stories of the torture. what did women do with their hair. where are the seers. what the hell does raw cotton feel like. bales & bales & generations of it.

it's just a mental journey

everyday terror slaps everyday people into niggahs on they
knees in streets at gunpoint. a sight i'm going to miss. no
lie. i will miss the varied tongues of downtown. echo park.
languid laziness of transported folks from texas low riding
commodified images thru south central's shifting borders.
maze of summer posturing down venice beach boardwalk.
phoney poverty chic of santa monica. silverlake gentrified.
peeping bodies compressed downtown.
& all the cafes newly spouted
black leather   queer nation politics
urgent homelessness
assault weaponry language   angry children
invisible segregation lines   exhaust fumes
& oh the pleasure tho' when i can look up the street on rare
days to see the hollywood sign cause it's just that clear cut
to sound my boots click against gorgeous sidewalks
walking from car door to car door fade to cool feat of
winding down sunset boulevard to ocean stage direction
see the car that just turned left in front of me that i
narrowly miss hitting cause that's what l.a. is it means to
narrowly miss your fate
& i must begin to say goodbye now or i may never leave

cross the great divide, she said

the way to the fair is roadblocked. desirous deciduous trees laugh. mystery lady feeds me a conditional intimacy. call. subvert laws of regret.
it was a beautiful concession.
the good men fell down dead.　stop.
it was a beautiful consent.
juggling clowns skating down main street. carnivals of violence bleach night air. firecracker. let the good times roll. mock. re-enter the danger zone. i live here to die there. i live here to survive in the out there. nobody listens to the believer. nobody senses the desperation of faith. everyone does. a body. naked to the open gaze. flagellate with instruments of chattel slavery. watch you come to the post pain ecstatic. answer the ringing. how come the ghost wail from chained histories. *how come we come.* everything permissible. clearing a mental jungle. desire. funny name for inhalation. my need to be held in flesh. *laugh you little ones.* your time of innocence is almost done. deliver me to a jesus believable. turn the water to wine. do your tricks for me. let the good times roll. latch that gate child. shut the house up good. all the bad people be waiting to violate the castle. rub some gentle on the lips chapped. *pussywillows.* she scratches the night. a beacon of pain or good luck. oh. don't you wanna walk like cool kids. snap in concert. play the game just to play. so honored to catch the dissolution of the twentieth century. *tonight we're going to party like it's nineteen ninety-nine.* i betray jealous gods. strain to hear angels sigh. earth runnings. every bit of it a fiction. this is the literal translation. i hurt a common love. my eyes forget to cry. i bleed to see you. i want love to be easy death. predictable somewhat linear.

she is more than useful fiction
(for danielle brazell)

divine you kiss my feet. miss you. a construction of flesh in
spirit. in eyes i don't live. pray. retrieve a sometime. go away.
i see the road to your face all the time. it's a family affair
said the machine. who said love is equal. retrievable against
all odds. who said love is this. oceans pass across wounds.
slipping in imaginative terrain a lady wants to exist in
woman form. don't tell nobody. you open the door never
to be the same again. known things escape. the magic is
not in the wand. which image more beautiful. *the one of*
you there beating yourself. the one of you there sleeping. the
one of you kissing the fear god on lips. one i made up in a
dream. now know a mutual topic. fathers parked on venice
beach. share a memory before parting. if i venture on the
tightrope. jump thru a safety net. lie in a known language.
there is nothing i want from you. lie. desire is not innocent.
a fax machine said desire is a bitch & i do desire you.
pretend away the need. confuse the emotion. what i want is
an obscene unable. what i want is not what i would give.
alchemist searching for a matchbook. sometimes god takes
on a face i'd recognize anywhere. sometimes. *droven.*
i believe any fiction you say. with fisted hands a little girl
pushes back a tear. a direct object of action. who could have
predicted the result. morning on a bed with a dog. naming
it doesn't reveal anything. in a dream. two women kiss in a
parking lot. better the beginning be the end.

summon, she said, her by the name you loved

what was i supposed to say. that love is a condition of the imagination. language makes things false. conditional and subject to agreement.

take me in like unopposed to mad currents of skin. kiss the darkness. pussy negotiable property. language a convenient construct. please do remember me. gospel and lost classics of the negro age. take me in. do lord remember me. remember me.

what was i supposed to say
the possibility of your breasts more enticing more beautiful than a threat of rain across hard earth. the scribes lost their way somewhere between the native wailing ghosts of new mexico and south carolina cotton fields. or was there sugarcane there. someone who knows should tell the urban black kids of uzi mtv and comic strip breakfasts. hail the gains of integration and cross the divide of race mythology. something is always lost when something is gained. who was prepared to pay the price for memory's transference from the sacred to the profane. from porkchops to mcdonalds. working backwards.

i supposed to say
the physical suck is never enough. moons have coalesced to confuse the day. take a slow train home. this is the long way. dissent. ahhh breath & feel better you radicals of steel. draw lines around the stomach that has birthed stretch marks. reject the smooth playboy image of femininity. lick.

how come you don't want to sleep with me anymore. this is the way to regret. don't answer now. save the reality for a day that can bear the weight. *i suppose i could have said love is a country of need & desire & the base resignation of leashes*. my flesh. all flesh. waiting to be materialized in touch. it aches. who has the money to buy a ticket to the second show. release me. then rescue me. charles brown on a.m. radio. *merry christmas baby, you sho' do treat me nice*. sing along. this tradition we'll name american for convenience.

intimate devils. *what to do when the outlaws are all in-laws*. the enemies you know by first name. consent and conquest. blackness. whiteness. oppositional bayonets. as if you and me embody incomparable mythologies. go girl. lick. in imaginative terrain you kiss my feet. i give you anything. & into this gaze that is not a gaze i saw nothing i want to name yet everything i want to claim. i want. selfish bitch i am. violating all twelve step rules. enable me & i'll enable you.

i say
you. beautiful in the overused meaningless way. not hideous enough to ignore. scratch. wish it all were the way the stories make it seem. who is parent of the false word. i am says the true confessor shackled in memory. feed the monster. these are beans & we have some chicken. what says pop culture. i loved you. through a gaze unholy & unrepentant. see me the girl i want to be. see me undressed. ribs decorated in skin. do lord remember me. reborn.

what was i supposed to say
that i loved you is too simple a lie. when i breathe your face
& see i am stunned with sight of you warrior girl your
wounds i want to cry in & suck blood. everything pales in
comparison. this is the secret of power. corruption so easy.
i want to sing a revolutionary song. dress in fatigue. kick
ass. lick pussy. did you say you are not black. you are not
white. create a theoretical language to situate the emotion.
i admit none of this. the exhibitionist just likes to expose
her scars.

pick any curtis mayfield song to accompany this

dance all night. sleep into sun. exhaustion as pedestrian
resistance. swagger of denial quite cute.
pathetic limp leaves falling off another
existence. cartoon street empty stillborn wish.
spasms of self. the margins have always been full.
a secret uncommercialized in advertisements.
& the taste of a porch sunken in north st. louis
leaves your lips blackened
as if a smoker's body were yours. was yours.
brick dilapidated structures. safety nets of disposables.
cool jerk. angry black man said. quiet man said.
quiet black man thick in eyeglasses said.
you want him to shout
eulogies at you. you want him to attack your guilt.
you want him to shut the fuck up. disappear into a statistic.
something to take seriously. understand. brother takes
possession of you though you make him biblical cain. somalia is
closer than watts so let's send the relief mission there. prioritize
oppressions. drink your coffee & don't think of the hands
that picked the beans. boycott grapes. anti-oppression
a series of hierarchies. like oppression. catch time
to pray on a crowded bus. keep the faith in face of bloated
eyes standing in the rubble that was a korean owned liquor store.
a particular historical reference. anger can be so arbitrary. or loyal.
abundant melanin makes no one holy. eat watermelon.
all the paths to blackness scattered in crystal shards.
somebody dies when the bullet hits. commercial break.
tell me the way to beauty christie brinkley. little black girl over
there crying in a corner cause little black boy said her lips too
big. they say in war there's lines clearly drawn.

never believe a man in uniform. kenya in military greens.
a cultural matter.
would you shoot me oh brother if my skin
were holy would you shoot me oh brother
if my skin were only mask would you shoot me oh sister
if the black myth survived madison avenue.
our own angers.

would you oh brother. walk holy with me through trash.
would you oh sister if i confessed the family name.

all the way to the fair the innocent child blows bubbles. little fatalities.
pick up a doll girl. learn the necessities of survival. braid its hair
& caress. call her yourself. evil is everywhere etched in minstrel.
dance. it's all right now. hold that brother's hand. dance.
it's all right now. think of ways feet crossed swamps.
give up the ghosts of easy blackness. i know what
the visionaries want. i was willing to buy.
the motherland myth. i want a way out too.

she said, talk to grandmother in cycles
(for mrs. bina bobo)

so this is what you ancients meant by crying time. i have
not been good. i have not been bad. sometimes i haven't
been nothing at all. grey haired lady. white haired lady.
perfect witch of high pitch. bathe me nice in kitchen sink.
general hospital plays in black & white. tears. all the
promises grew up. be a good lady. hey lady. he ain't never
coming back that blond haired jesus now is he. if i see death
first i'll tell him to treat you good. if you see him first tell
him to let me hang out with you. feathery clouds. i put most
of the coins in the gold tinted tin plate for you. the others
went for soda pop. hope you don't mind my minor
transgressions. white haired lady. where your rifle at now.
cataract eyes. i'll try to shoot straight. be unafraid. never
bury half my children. never promise lofty world trips
again. weep. b.b. king & lucille shudder in overstuffed
rooms. picture albums. junk antiques. precious all of it you
precious in a retrospect too late. snow at winter's edge. my
momma a big bird flew away to sun. come on in now. it's
getting on time for supper. y'all. tablecloth. i want pork again
& i want it now. negroes & nostalgia. i never heard you sing.
i never saw you cry. cackling hen's laugh. spit that snuff
straight. i am trying to be as honest as grief will allow. i am
trying to be saved. i am trying to sin. i am trying to hush
these tears. *hush. somebody's calling my name.*

she said,

you come to a place where your eyes need to cry
they cry
dry river beds
how did you break your heart
how did you refuse your spirit a body
she said, you where to find her
she hangs like a beaten broom
at the I-10 freeway entry with sign pleading
tell your rage hello
forest moves in december
there were good witches in aphrodisiac trees
they said i won't let you go
i kneeled a catholic girl's submission
i said i want
i want the way to myself

is you is or is you ain't

nobody's home in my body. morning come hurriedly here.
zoom past the vehicles. menstrual blood turns some boys
on. groom the poodle. guess i forgot to turn the denial
faucets off last night. wicked highway beating time. over.
emptied of pleasure. crass flowers. miniature men painted
in combat green. line them up to watch them die. order is
what i like. all the files labelled. the desire for one more
round. roar down street like the other tourists. say prayers
then go home. somalians in bloated stomach costumes
wrecking my panafrican day. happy is the password. stretch
out on the underside of a void. clean dream. thank god
somebody's keeping time. all the girls started on their way.
little ones & big ones & white & pink knee socks. preen in
the mirror & silence my lips. pop. fly away home. ed sullivan
introduces diana ross. & the supremes. done to the tune of
deceit. how can you love me like that. put those flaws on
the table. she said baby girl. you got it. she said. gin.
shoeboxes full of dope. by the way. off went the big dick.
exploding for small change. give me this daily bread. i wants
to eat. so i lied again. it's only between me & you. right.
what does it matter. i'm going to amsterdam with my wig
screwed on tight. all my friends gonna sing background.
off & off & off. click. wait for that moment of recognition.
staple the pages shut. strokes of midnight walk tensely by.
go back to start. look surprised at the trickery. again. such
faith keeps me going. god loves us don't you know child.
comfort. i could have sworn it was her on the street. it was
her on my page. it was her true form stretched across my
bed. her left breast on my lip. nipple reddish brown.
galaxies skipping over my stretch marks. dreams. they got
me. how are you.

under the bedspread, those smells, maybe nobody will notice

all the children have that little white lamb to follow them to school. lumber past construction workers perched. gypsy in their souls. they'll learn to masturbate to be better persons. redeem their food stamps for discount meat. yelp goes the dog kicked. this is a paid holiday. assemble. now swallow those bitter pills like good girls & boys. kinky goes the future. sit bare assed on sun. get those labia & penis pierces now. pain's the way for you to go. forgive your mothers all their dissuaded fantasies & burnt aspirations. put the erect nipple between your teeth. bite hard & the screams turn sultry. smile little ladies. little gents. big daddy loves you sho' nuff. it's not your decomposed bodies strung up in effigy. you're all going to disneyland.

so where do you enter memory

then in the personal world myths were grudges. a fairytale. i invent. swallow the discontent. eat. a new form of abuse. all the divine twists dent fate's narrow corridor. ghosts drip semen from vinyl seat impalas. cool music on radio. mellow dirty nails. the touch. fingers on flesh of the baby in the tub in the sink in the house once new now falling mercilessly upon itself. regurgitated snuff crashes into her tin can. martha & the vandellas sing harmony in background. poof. who said it was never there. go away. any way. i need to fuck myself in such a way that the moans eat me alive. no witnesses. church hats. round boxes stuffed in closets. my mother told me i was a girl. i wanted to call her god but the timing never seemed right. falling to mortality all the time. grievers need a black gal's moody red. now all rise. in the marketplace of dreams isis found osiris' penis. fragmented. i want a myth that would not explain some thing. to enter the church doors on my knees. i want jesus to fill me up. want the holy ghost to shout in tongues. want to fuck in the pulpit. i want you to look at my scars & be healed. contemporary martyrdom. statues of lenin line streets of a melted iron curtain. uprooted dogma. give me a simpler slogan. all the ideologies have faded into dusty corners. musty hardbound editions of unread books line shelves. go away little boy. marlena shaw sang it sweet. waiting to be born. i won't doubt myself against the image of the madonna. we share the same secret of blood & blood & blood. the holy. the god. the woman vaginal fluids. the need to suckle breast. the clutching vulva. the inner lips. screams as heads of baby ghosts push out. the mystery of flesh. there's another little tether ball queen   girl muscles on an asphalt smooth playing field. step on a crack. your mamma real black. this is not where i thought we were going to when we got on the train. all the seats were taken. we caught a phoenix fleeing the burning kuwaiti oil fields which rode us all the way to kansas city. i saw 1948 in monochrome & all the ears were full with jazz. men danced their hats at cool angles. shoes two toned stacy adams. primal kitchens & the myth of black culture went unrecognized in everyday realms. in some small space of my everyday body where i live. with all the genetic ghosts & other intruders embedded in my spine.

lover, she says, dare you hold my sorrow

rain streaks blood down river. gushing teenagers in love carpool thru. your eyes go away from me. simple pleasures. breasts to breasts. i thought danger would be more dangerous. i thought my thoughts could summon a wish into being. roller coasters spiralling off track. city. this one. a creation in disassembly. smash the mirrors & turn off the light. she journeyed into blood river for me. would you. lover dare you hold my my psychic twists. what name is that i answer to. credible lies. generous is the hand that pats the infant master's head. how do i recognize you in crowed pastels. click. whisper it like you mean it. sincere as first kiss. i come to laughter willingly. say amen. double clap. let the organ moan. hide. patrollers bark in little gestapo boots at the door. your therapist or my pot. why choose crutches. surely we can have them all. next world. don't you see something gracious is happening here. i've seen people dunked in holy water to come up the same. angels took me over cliff. spectacular fall. clearly earth is a bed of roses. stick a tongue into the thorns.

she says

where in the world are all the acid queen poplar trees the willow like a lady beautiful & stupid in her distress weeping on a stolen pillow the redwoods singing grace at dawn the weed stumped growth in a patch between here & there & the neighborhood falls asleep to the lull of a redundant poppopopopopoptatatatat daffodils shifting earth's axis cool spearmint freelancing in suspended gratitudes to a god who looks like any woman's sister keeper looks i would keep her away from pain's blank stare.

she says the bar is dirty & the big boys & girls have gone to another time zone. she says shame. she says on a good night you can hear incoming fantasies hijacked aboard the concord. she says we are the ones our mothers warned us about. ain't it nice to be noticed. she said button your pants. she says who's got money for another drink. she said the love is too much an absence. she says sit yourself down & tell me some secrets if you please. she says pass the hotsauce. she says the world is my friend. she says pull the covers tighter around me. she says we are the ones we've been waiting for. she says sit right down & talk to me. i cannot move. thank you for the beer.

simple language. girl woman out of bounds. nappy night sweats caressing sheets. sweet. cyclonic cross references spinning lullabies lovely as lingering watermelon juice sitting pretty on the soul's terrain. somebody scat. twist like you did last night. jump the broom & bring it all back home. turn on the heat. simple language. the delicate eyelashes sweep thru clouds.

free me up.
the party's been fun & i wanna go home.
the world's been kind to me & i wanna go home.
the niggahs on my block treat me nice & i wanna go home.
the good hosts are gracious as they can be & i wanna go
home. the food it's cooked to taste spicy & i wanna go home.
the mood gorgeous nostalgic sepia & i wanna go home.
the black hats look nice on the heads and the shoes match
the purses fashion slick announcements of credibility & i
wanna go home.
the walk is nice thru the foreign lands & the words are
sphinx mysteries to entice tongue & i wanna go home.
& i wanna

saturday, she says

(for laura meyers)

rush hour. it rained the day i drove away. first in weeks
months maybe. bye bye girls it's time to put the tape in the
car radio and ride. boom into quiet. gravel and time crunch
under wheels. don't stop. keep going. the future is still the
future and promise seems sweet. l.a. a slick piece of burnt
toast soggy in the rain. and if the sun is shining while it's
raining then the devil is beating his wife that's what this
girl said on the playground one day ago i was little and
playing it happened the devil started beating his wife i
wondered if she was beautiful and what he looked like. i
said i bet she was the sun. echo park your studio
apartment overtaken by weighty desk and pullman bed
lumpy mattress and no pillows for sleeping on because you
said your mother said pillows throw your head out of
alignment with your body. you giggle when you come. then
like that everything makes sense the water catching its
breathe the droning lawn mower the cars going by the
singer the song the rush and nothingness of the days.

she said, meditate on rage

i am falling. i am falling. i fall into the crawl spaces of the androgynous witches who scream bedtime lullabies at my bruised teeth.
i am going. i am going. i am going into the coven of lesser stars where the pain cannot find me. and there is nothing romantic about death there. i said hello but the jackal spirit screamed back in scorn that i don't know its name. i don't know its name. so why masquerade a modest empathy devoid of a real object.

oh how does this rage find me. i try so hard to disappear into the happy.
where do the lucky ones live. i want to eat at their table.

i am dancing. i am dancing. i dance off the edge of the girlwoman who dresses in my ashy skin. i sing. i am singing. i am singing goodbye. who said that for every ending there's a beginning. i like that lie.

i said love me please could you do that for me baby just for tonight like some sacred radio song we could snuggle up together and kiss & shit and whisper things in one another's ears that we will never forgive ourselves for believing and our skins will float naked and shaved and imperfect and orgasmic and baby huh baby huh could you do that for me could you do that with me could you do that to me just for one night

i am inventing. i am inventing. i am inventing a woman who i can let live in beauty inside of me. i am forsaking. i forsake myself. the scarred scared bitch who answers to my name is just too hard to bear.

speak in the two voices

execute the cruelty beautifully you are released no passive voices here in the sadist dance i release you cut the exterior ego into dust into apple slices into an exquisite blood unavailable in emergency rooms we aren't angels i saw the angel there in your bed we aren't goddesses i saw the goddess there in the bathroom stall in the golden flush of your eyes these realities speak in dualities split the skull open i need to see the residual cartoon the roadrunner incredible death defyer in black and white can you make me cry try can you expose the fear of my truth here's my thumb stick in the knife an expert surgeon can cut to the death zone then sew back up the voluntary slavery who's got the power the good slave or the bad master or the good master or the bad slave i know where you want to go i know what you want i love your fears i love your power are you precious in sleep awakening to the unknown dreams my sweet baby breathe all over again my lips are so

wound to the life zone go girl golden haired distress pop i love you my mother is a good woman bitch bow bitch what does power respect but power what does power need to destroy but the mirror power this is bullshit how we wish this is memorable performance there is the stage directions maimed in my eyes there's the program to hand to the audience crying on a phone machine i love life let's die now it might never again be such a gorgeously hard time to live slave i bend easily before your pussy a confession booth in which i can kiss goddesses and demons in unequal and unquestionable devotion no one's getting out now the machine is always on call when you can i have ice for the bruise may i use your bathroom i hear the brave revolutionaries are preparing another coup to save the world again i'm so tired of war girls just wanna have fun

parched   don't dare kiss them
they cut the sky's sanity into little
blue candles to burn into the
night's black   black cats and
black unborn and black magic
and black delight go now you
are released   where in the
planetary evolution should i
meet you to embark on the next
chapter of the her and her story

tell me a story, she says

into the inner reaches of the vulva fantasies. go there now into what is liquid and solid and holds all truth. my goddess waits for me in a debried alley. little goddess of sanity. i like to see your ass exposed to sun. in this alley strewn with streamers of lost parades & cadillac hub caps & eunuchs' bodies and such shit. i don't go there to meet her. i send my illusion self instead. her knees visible in the torn jeans. my illusion floats down to her. my lips her lips kiss. she entices with her red smear even now you can see her laughing in lipstick advertisements. i kneel before her supplicant and unafraid of consequence. my tongue licking haints and ghosts from her snake hair.

it is so dark in here daddy. when i kneel before her the severed penis falls from my back pocket. it is so much light in here daddy. i hear the voice of my sister muffled under the bedspread.

i dream that a contingent of white doves are coming from the castle to save me. and a gift of angels is on its way to climb through the barred windows to name me. and all the little hopscotch queens are armed on playgrounds to protect me. please. please says the little girl wrapped in her patent leather shoe protection. please love me. please says the big man. it is so dark in here and the house is haunted and cannonball adderley and mr. miles davis are reaching for holiness on the reel to reel tape. please says the big man tied up in fishnet stockings as a steel cross brands his chest. please says the big man tied to the corporate marble table as his tongue is sliced out. please says the penis warped in the girls mouth. please touch me. my goddess kneels on the alley floor with me. her bare knees suck in the broken bottle glass.

why do you bleed for me i ask. she laughs and golden streams leak from her mouth. i don't bleed for you she says. i bleed for me for you to witness.

and i think i hear my sisters muffled screams emerging from the bedspreads. and i think the world is giving out lollipops to all the good girls. and i think i hear her sighing ahhhh. she pulls my pants down. her tongue goes into the black pink of my inner lips. why do you cry little one. i am so afraid daddy. soldiers are at the front gates pointing their guns. priests ask for a confession. the mother has hidden her face behind make-up. how come they won't teach the baby to walk. sweet goddess holds the baby in mortal form. we pass air between the space of our lips. her fingers rubbing my clitoris into erection. tell me a story of once upon a time a queen loved a whore and a saint kissed the devil and silk sheets lined the earth's roughness and a woman danced her tongue over my tears. tell me daddy. i am so little but the mystery is so big. my legs are scorched joints keeping time to the good music. where are your gods now my goddess and i laugh as we stick the knife into the big man's groin. where is your power now we moan as her fingers file polyrhythms in and out of my pussy. make believe. when i grow up i'm going to be an assassin daddy. when i grow up i'm going to be a healer daddy. when i grow up i'm going to remake a lie daddy when i grow up i'm going to become a bird daddy when i grow up i'm going to bleed. when i grow up i'm going to kneel in a forgotten alley with a goddess and harps and flutes and electric guitars and belts and whips and burning logs and frozen nipples and severed penes and trolls and tricksters and ghosts are going to make a party.

abcdefg won't you come and play with me.

sanctified suck of redemption i kiss her breasts milk sweet as fetus innocence. you can bite me she says i am goddess and all pain is transparent. i rub my hands on her ass you can spank it she says i am goddess and all pain is redemption. i lick my tongue across the shadows of her face you can cut it she says i am goddess and every slice aids in my transformation into all things beautiful. i hand her the severed penis. why don't they teach the baby to walk. her knees are swollen menses. she crawls. crawl little one. learn to love in supplication my goddess says to me. i see her my mirror self. she holds the severed penis in her mouth. i am lightness and air and the weight of a thousand feathers lying across her naked back. glitter. blood of our broken knees mark our path. penis between her teeth leaks succulent petals of stolen flowers falling and merging into the blood. she bites. i am on her back. my pussy is swollen afterbirth rubbing against my goddess' bare ass mine exposed beautiful and petulant to sun. stigmatas adorn our hands.

my goddess raises her hands to my face. i lick off the blood. are you ready she whispers. up towards the blind. buildings below stacked   play form in a child's design. climbing up we squeeze tightly into each other. the goddess i open our mouth allowing the penis to disintegrate into fragments of its power. the goddess i call out to the little girl in an attic in a house whose clitoris is shackled to a man's penis in a town in a time nameless. don't cry little one the goddess i say. bite.

come to me when you can't speak she said

you remember the cataclysmic night for what it is. what it was. how do i appreciate the gift you gave for winter. it bites my shoulder in crack pipe denouements. we went into the field of sky virgin mistresses. we went into the winter in skins of distress and rebirthed placenta. place your lips here on this wound. i am so afraid. this is a truth that speaks its sister's name. why do i know her as i know myself. we went into winter. how do i thank you for the warmth placed behind your left ear lobe. you invited me to taste prophetic cancers. i am your witness. i don't give up the voice of sight. though it chokes in an anger so common even i am ashamed to recognize it as my own. what do i want. so many more winters.

what do i want. so many more winters.

what do i want. so many more winters.

what do i want.

you in so many more winters.

as if the gift were not enough.

this day is upon me in darkness. i weigh a burden of recrimination fool wrapped in supplication. there was star. a mountain. a laughter. a woman. a tattoo. there is no way to anoint the mystery within this memory. she gave me the gift of winter and spring left me so unfinished. a bastard child clinging to window ledge. how do you say thank you naked and shivering in the lost time. i recognize you. i recognize you. you held me over the ice. i held you near magic acid trees under some clear cold stars.

she said, again

i'm not jealous just afraid of losing. never seem to beat
anyone to the punch. my good girl. hide behind the
telephone ring. water passes down a narrow opening in the
cliff falling to its birth five hundred feet down. shipwrecked
on a city street i see what i cannot say. be afraid. look over
someone's shoulder for the answer. dear abby. what should
i do to apologize. if there were words i would say sorry. but
we've fled language. our bodies dangle in the absent space.
talk to silence. it answers in tongues even a retired christian
could decipher. when the going gets rough i'm going to hold
my child and rock. i wanted carrot juice but things just don't
seem to come up daisies. twist. let me in on the joke. look
my mouth can laugh. what is a sensible murder. wrong
answer. say your prayers aloud. make sure god hears you. i
know which boundary i've blundered. your love is your
own & not mine. if we were older we would have played
the game right. but we are so young we don't even know
how to tie up the frayed edges of this rope. i want to beg
forgiveness but i heard only men do that. girlfriends just
retire to separate rooms to sew patches on the holes.

the grass is always greener, she said

in this season of dreams trees bend to kiss my ear. i come into winter virginal & unafraid of cold. suicides a faraway tale shored against an ocean i love. welcome to 1993. i hear everyone's dysfunctional. i hear they're the best they can be. stand in line. gorgeous repressed bellies pulled tight on a string. sip. which way is the five & dime. generous is your hand the one that extends the tobacco for free. feed me another promise. do you think they'll come to the party. balance carefully on the slippery banks of forever where's that at. a storefront pretending to be east fourteenth in a time of better revolutionary assumptions. say who dat who love me. in this season of dreams i walk into an alley on the good side of the street a man pushed her head through a plate glass window. think good thoughts now and good shall come to you. i think i left my patience at the express line but i really don't remember. are you making up another story. the prim teacher bends down to the little child forced to silence.

she said, own it

find me here in the oversized room where the bad girls go
to kneel. look into another mirror for answers. too tired to
know what i know. confess on another sunday. they'll come
again with the assurance the arrogant devise as some sort
of destiny. a town waits for me to arrive. dream a
comfortable fiction. i'm with you all the way. two women
in a dance of connective tissue. we are. i walked once
through dangerous skyscraper tonguing the moon. slow
drag of feet search for a resting place. there was a song but
the words escape me now. like all good movies the ending
came out good. the heroine died. i don't remember my lines.
say this to the body curled alone under a pile of blankets.
winds claw at inadequate window panes. say that. you say
this to say what. just don't say what i can't believe. boogie. i
didn't know where i was going but i was sure when i
arrived that it was the right place. seven years this walk
through the angers. home. a pillow lies beneath my eyes.
catching the wet doubts so sweet.

she said, don't give up

pleasure to be here earthling in this time of seductive tears staining the ground of our planet. so much work to be done now. children demystifying broken homes. a new road travelled so many centuries before. lovely the snow stuck to that mountain beyond the suburban roof. eat. the complexity is not so much that someone is starving at the instant we come into joy. but that we can come into joy while someone is starving. can my pleasure feed someone's emptied protruding belly. how did that mystic turn the water to wine. turn the words to bread. turn the bread to spirit. it is the revolutionary imperative of this age. to be alchemist. to play god in a script rewritten and divulged of unelected leaders. the bad men are knocking on the front door. we can't ignore them while we wait to collect on our historicized rape. palestinians are not getting all their land back. native american indians are not getting north america. colorado won't be new spain again. forget the 40 acres and a mule. paraphrase. jones turned baraka was right when as jones he said he is like any other sad man here. american. the queen is dead. the british royal family a tabloid anachronism. power won't yield to idealism. quests for beauty. we know that now.

we know their guns are bigger than ours. we have the same old dumb shit voodoo we've always had. faith sung in work lines. i believe in the dumbshit voodoo. i believe that faith will carry us through. i believe the earth loves to live. i believe that oprah will marry steadman and live happily ever after. i believe that the ability to live in faith is the backbone against repression. that resistance is worth more than collection on the debt owed. i believe that the forces of good will kiss evil on lips. it is simple moments like this that gives me the strength to stand in the unemployment line with dignity. bear the offhand bark of a chained pet. plot everyday subversive acts against the death state. to know that planting collard greens matters. that words are not frivolous. & freedom is more than just some people talking.

tressles of hair, she said

then there was a girl who fell in love with a girl & said this is a love that can speak its name. one girl said we will tell them when they ask for a definition of relationship that i am your white slave bitch and the other girl she laughed she felt it was an appropirate twist of an appropriation. we want a world that sustains our base desires. multitudes chorus. clap. we want a world that transcends the wailing shackled ghosts real as depression and apple pie. *how do you feel what they say is not permissible to feel.* wicked ladies and wild men and good cultural workers doing the stuff of transformation. at the deli counter ordering tuna on rye. death and rebirth. natural matrix of mortality. where that god be at. come to me now on a cross of extended clitori budding in want of suck. *i'm not bad.* the little girl has on a white tee shirt. she sits in the polaroid picture frame innocent as any make believe. write this down or the past may forget its part in the current. draw the line somewhere says a smart woman from the t.v. screen. in the car the girl into the girl girl thing said behind her eyes in a language unnecessary to voice she said she wanted to eat your breasts now she wanted to suck your lips now she wanted to fuck you for redemption and scream into the vortex of breathless space where thighs shudder.

she said, talk to grandmother in cycles: cycle 3

stay with me a moment. there is a dream i forgot to tell. a
dream i forgot to forget. what is it in remembrance that
shrieks me awake. the night alone in its shell sitting there
wide eyed as the woman who is the girl who travelled into
a valley. old black woman in church hats weird as velveeta
cheese perched on straightened hair home done. i know
their eyes without looking. i know their voices and the crack
of their bones and the feet that carried the day's weight in
thick stockings and sensible shoes. stay here for a moment
and pretend the urgency of their lives is bound to ours.
prayers they say from lips perched in royal resistance.
afro-delight. *they say from blackened lips that we are child.*
that we are child in continuum of a blackness that recognizes
us in rebirth and despair. they say child. sit down. rest for
awhile. they say child. who your people be. child. what your
people's name. is you somebody's child. in the valley of these
souls. song. have you heard that song broken like the fairy
tale house the little pigs stood in against the big bad wolf.
eat. sweet potatoes glazed over. salt the food right. there is
some trick to standing in the valley unharmed. to singing
the song broken into asphalt under the green go light
invented by one who we call our own. i can't tell you their
fears the ones who know the songs. i could tell you of their
hands. the callouses. smooth hard leathered harnesses
pulling centuries of field workers nappy heads knockkneed
ashy legs into the blinding vortex of a north star somebody
done told them it would light their way. i could tell you
about faith. i could tell you about girdles and clasped hands.
i could tell you about the heavy iron of the hot comb molded
into the fabric of these black calloused hands. i could tell

you of seared ears. i might simper out hymn. but i couldn't tell you of their fear. in the valley fear is a fool's defense. fear is a boat. fear is a choice. i could tell you something of how they chose to live against fear. how the kitchen smells graced their eloquent lips that would elicit a laugh. deep pungent vasoline oiled hands that leaned into your face cupped like flower. a kiss on the plaited braids. an unassuming intentional act taken for granted. i could tell you of the valley. how it looks. stay with me longer here. this dreamscape is not forbidden. this dream calls to be spoken. i can tell you of purples and yellows. knots and braids. i could tell you that the valley is wide and long but i am not really telling you the mystery. i could tell you of the floating world. i could tell you of these practitioners of the floating world. i could tell you how the people learned to fly. *when i walk thru the valley i shall fear no one.* i could sing that. i could tell you. of the goings and comings. of train rides north. of little girls in their best dresses in 1964 eating chicken on a passenger train delivering them to grandmother's house. i could tell you that it is a sister to holiness this faith is.*take my hand. lead me on.*

she said, sometimes love's rage will just eat you alive, won't it?

once i was tricked by a crystal's bright glare like it was valuable self reconstruction. a way to find some peace in the forest of self induced weakness. the imposter said she was a friend of the darkness. the imposter said lots of things no one cared to repeat.
i don't know how to sit in this shame more regally than the demented shadow of her will allow.   how to make the bitter aftertaste leave me.
what is this bitch of fear riding the waves around my chest. what is this. a tear. sweet vagina juices gallop down my cheek. a savior that won't say its name.
this is not what i wanted to hurt. a displacement evading definitions.

mock a rude soft *h* consonant. try to form the words that would say home & cats come out screeching in the streets with claws drawn. smashed apricots rot on an abandoned sidewalk. the rapists' semen pushes into chaotic basements where dead girls lie. corpses waiting for some undertaker to name their true form. bring on the death hearse if you dare. like i'm too proud to take my seat. i can open my own doors too.
did you ever cast a shadow on the sun. cry cause all the light was gone.
did you ever betray a dream. worse the dream maker.
did you ever sock yourself with all your strength and didn't feel it.
i thought the apple was some other vegetable.
i don't know the ways of love.

i don't know what love is.
i came to the fair to play. i didn't know i'd be thrown from the rollercoaster. i forgot what it feels like to fall. is this some outstanding debt i forgot about. is this how the arrogant die. sitting straight up in a bed of choice. all the channels clicked to off. the scent of someone you dared called lover still fragrant in pillowsheets. one lone bird sings beyond the sliding doors. grief clogging the sinuses. the kick ass girl bound and tied into silence. the mother a failed bitch again.

cross the line, she said

don't enter here. don't come in here. this place where the
hard wound of hate eats. you are not welcome into this pain
you've brought. fine wounded bitch hardened beside
curbside rain puddle. give another gift please. print this
image on glossy slick magazine paper. i am not without
fault. i loved too hard. beautiful singer man he said *his
friends sometimes say. but i believe*. i believe. that a woman
should be. is this the rage you meant to find behind
curtain number one. the sorceress sleeps. light the match.
who burns first. freaks on knees on floor on bathroom hard
on ass orifice on lips on sleeping sickness on
poppopopopopop die beautiful one like children. falling. a
swing empty in the false park. *push me push me* they cry.
little ghosts.

she said, treasure it

in the morning your face. a garland for me. the way your eyes drape the shadowed morning. a beat. a slip. a suck. a flesh memory. bodies of two women emerged in the unfolding of a mystery. this one. skins contrast. laugh in a recreated space of blacks and whites. psychedelic freak out. sacred pussy water. taste it sweet. collective solo incantations scream. cajoles niggah gods. nubian goddesses. two toned cadences grind a slow dance into magic.
see how your fingers are alchemists.
i was mortal & earth bound redundancy. your touch it says fly here. your lips on mine they say this magic place is fragrant in popsicle tears. you can cry into my flesh. the pain won't hurt. then your eyes they said come. look precious one. you float before the golden gods on stolen rafts of tears. how the sun worships the lovely ones. who goes into the frozen river alone to search the ice for friends. it is the time of a new letting go. i can't bow before the end of the world arrives. set the table. gandhis and kings and crack heads are coming by. my mother wants the stolen jewels of her life back. pawned in her overly made up eyes. i want to love you but the words keep getting in the way. i want to place myself in a shrine as offering

she said, heather

you run your hand through this forest. black pubic hair.
penetrate the fears. tickle tongue over generations of
stubborn women. ecstatic surrender. it's time to play. take
me to the place where you go when there is no separation
between the whip & the lick. commodified postcards.
lotus afloat in ponds fragrant. i am a beggar on the path
dressed in fine threads. i bend over to receive the power
you steal so fine your. shoplifted hands. say your hidden
name. release the shame housed in your pussy. turn up the
lights. this is not the time for darkness to obscure your face
a mask violet in trumpet hues.

The Absence of the Lover Makes Her Who She Is

(for cynthia davis)

"The sky behaved like a showgirl."
from *Paradise*, Toni Morrison

1.

She came to greet me earth-filled with tall tales of
black-eyed peas and pig ear sandwiches.
She came with shining pots, shrimp, pasta.
She say whatchumacallit then kiss me with lips of carmex
chap stick.
She say loved-ed. She say unlessen.
She say dis den dat den she kiss me on my forehead right
above the bicycle scar.

2.

Contours of light and shadowed cheekbones rise like mist
on morning light accentuating pillow cover.
smell of papaya sleeps in drain when there's been
no tropical allusions in this kitchen for over a year.
Window blinds drawn against alien creep traffic outside.
Inside a private site of dream.
Her. Cheekbones. Risen northern star guiding hidden
impulse. Vulvar light.
Black dust powder licks nipples. I once hallucinated her in
an imagined version of love.
Luminous scar rides the left side of her stomach up to the
rib cage of her. I kiss.
She sleeps in the shape of Texas. A mirror shows her body

back to me. Black hair. Black eyes.
Black public hair. Skin the color of a smooth brown
cashmere sweater I could have worn when I was younger,
window shopping in the rain in Brooklyn.

3.
Window shopping in the rain once in Brooklyn.
Folsom street offered me a discount emotion. Folsom street
a dehydrated assault of psyches.
Pedestrian refractions shadow retail windowpanes,
passing, preening, pause.
What's love got to do, got to do with it. I learned to say
boombox and pointed at one in a cramped electronics store.
(a longing, longed for love)

4.
Consider touch the closest thing we have to manifesting
the divine. Flesh as terrain. As in: in the beginning there
was matter so supple it melted the mind's body.
Love as a practiced, particular thing less imagined than
pronounced,
consciously constructed. Peppermint lipstick flavor on a
slight moon mouth.

5.
Declawed tiger voice slipping. Slips. When you coming this
way again girl? I confuse the leaving with the dreaming.
Stalled in a theory of want. Me a subject of my woman who
is out of reach. I dream myself the subject of her out of
reach. What do you show, when called upon to show

yourself, loved one? A weeping willow stands in a bed of limegreen Kool-Aid. Her dancing dark eyebrows, my woman who is out of reach. What is it that you want child? Her. And more than what my limited imagination can conjure up. Daintiness in ways it is sometimes disguised: coarse negro fingertips drifting over a bowl of scented water, rose or sage medicinal. Lace in a flutter of wind gentling down the broad hips of a blueblack big, big woman dressed all in white. On her way to the fair perhaps. My woman perhaps. Walking away from our lazy big old front porch.

Lover: I

what the body remembers. it was not that complicated. the history.
divisions.   cut-ups.   intrigues.
a tattoo on the upper right flank where the skin bears   witness. a rose.
emblazoned there a lost lover's shadow. an old script.
dilapidated desire. what becomes fact. a factual encoding. a tussle's negotiated
outcome.
            more difficult. what was that
song she used to lisp.   it sounded raw silk.
michael row the boat ashore. how the whip courted the flesh.   his dowry.
a truckload of straightening combs & transitive verbs.
skin cancer is very very
rare in the african american community. therefore it's hard to remember. the sun.
come on over here and kiss me baby. she wanted to show how place traps
consciousness. how men write histories. I thought she would look nice
dressed in her father's battered face.
the kenyan coffee in the cup stained the african colonial map.   I spilled.
            how come you don't never buy me nothing I could pawn.
she acted like it hurt.   at the moment it happened I didn't mean it
when it was over.   she wanted to talk.
I don't remember the royal dutch trading company.
yes she insisted. yes you do. *michael rowed the boat ashore.*
come over here to the green futon. sit on my lap. they came in droves.
I don't remember.
come over here.   it was before the new millennium she said.
don't you remember they sung *hallelujah.*
I dreamed you took me to jamaica.   we slept on sand.
your dead cousin hustled us in montego bay.   we paid him store bought
cowrie shells to take us to (ethiopia) haile selassie's shrine. my ear wouldn't
stop bleeding.
your dead cousin said they have a word for this kind of female insurgency.

your politics slipped from my labia on the boat ride across the bay.
you thieved your mouth away when you saw him looking.   as if seared.
as if suddenly feeling the text.   you seemed ashamed of what he saw.
they have a banishment for *lesbian* in our language he said. I don't remember.
he wouldn't remember to tell us.   you thought we spoke english.
you said *I thought we were speaking in english*.   for fifty
american dollars he would service both american tourist ladies.
you insisted we talk about algae.

       or eighteenth century insurgency in the outlaw hills of Accompong.
   your dead cousin insisted on cash. at the moment of inquiry you could not
recall my name.
no not lover.   they have another marker for it. a subjective reading.
duplicitous experience.
that was a *duplicitous experience* you said when we got off.

Lover: II

no not that part.   the part that made sense. like when your mother
called you
The Tramp.   yes that part. the other childhood.   yes that one.
she was a poet then. she said something like
come into the night of mindless chambers.
see the disordered beauty prancing in straight lines.
that was before the collard greens finished
cooking.   sympathetic. we were going on a drive.
through the country. orange groves they leaned into the car window.
you thought there was a scarecrow.   we weren't in
massachusetts. you must have disremembered. yes. that's it.
I have disremembered.
the laughter caught in sunrise's humidity. we must have been someplace other
than here.
by the fence the little boy said when the devil tries to make me do things I don't
want to, I just say
no.   I didn't have that childhood. I was always a bird with a long blue tail
pecking unripened green apples on the highest branch. that's
   what you said on the drive.   my lips weren't kissing yours.
the lipstick smears you said. smears the lip's outline like an out of tune violin.
if that's all you wanted you should have
   said so.   that was all I wanted.
a few words maybe. some souvenir to put on the mantel for later.
like when all this is over.
what you experience is your valid reality.   you said *pretentious.*
I was too pretentious to be included. for some reason you made
this a personal scene.   not the distance required of nonfiction.
like when your mother sang you a nursery rhyme.
        twinkle twinkle little star. how I wonder what you are.
I thought your teeth were edible.

hello hello I echoed against you. *you simply the best*. that's what I meant to
say. we drove to nantucket. that made you laugh. we saw *jane run*. *mittens*.
they lived in a different storybook.   I disremember.
it was the blue shirt with the bleach marks on it.
in the closet in kentucky I kissed it. you wore it to the pool table.
you've never been to kentucky. that's what you said.
I used to think it cute the way you invent
but it bores me now.   that's what I would have said.
4 oz. olive oil + oil of rosemary & 5
drops oil of lemongrass. my mother washed my hair in the kitchen sink.
you told me that while waiting for the B bus to boulder.
      this is the part where my hand grabs your throat.
            voicebox rumbles through california. *be more exact, that's what*
you said. you pretty.
dorothy dandridge ankles and esther phillips skin. they lived in *Ebony*.
on the coffeetable that's where your mother left them out for company
that never came.
the sofa wasn't green. we were on our way to a party on divisidero street.
my mother died giving birth to me. you said it without any emphasis.
I believe it was vienna.
we bathed breasts together in a porcelain tub. my mother took me to
disneyland on my fifth. birthday.
I loved you the way you said it with certainty.
yes, when I was five.

Note from the editors

Akilah warped time and space. Akilah stretched every label there is. Akilah changed every room she entered. Akilah chased the ecstatic, rapture. Akilah seized her desires, seized life. Akilah's literary and performance work is brilliant, timeless. Akilah is brilliant, timeless.

These are just some of the things that come to mind when we think about our dear sister and friend Akilah Oliver, some of the things that gathered us together to bring *the she said dialogues: flesh memory* back into print.

Akilah Oliver (1961-2011) was born in St. Louis and grew up in Los Angeles. In 1994, she co-founded the experimental, feminist performance collective Sacred Naked Nature Girls, whose multiracial participants explored what Akilah called *flesh memory*, uncontainable transhistorical, trans-spiritual memories and trauma and desires activated in and through the body and its languages. Flesh memory returns in her stunning first book of poetry, *the she said dialogues: flesh memory,* which was published in 1999 by Anne Waldman's Smokeproof Press/Erudite Fangs Editions and received a PEN Beyond Margins award, and which appears here, reprinted.

Akilah's work with flesh memory continues in her second book of poetry, *A Toast in the House of Friends* (Coffee House, 2009). This searing book embodies the aporia of Akilah's far-too-many grief experiences, particularly the death of her son Oluchi McDonald in 2003 at age 21. After this tragedy, Akilah started the LINKS Community Network to fight for universal healthcare in honor of Oluchi, who was an accomplished graffiti artist and whose graffiti tag was LINKS. *A Toast* includes an essay on graffiti art and several poems that are scores which Akilah performed with various musicians and artists.

Akilah also published several chapbooks, including *An Arriving Guard of Angels, Thusly Coming to Greet* (Farfalla Press, 2004), *The Putterer's Notebook* (Belladonna* Books, 2006), *a(A)ugust* (Portable Press at Yo-

Yo Labs, 2007) and *A Collection of Objects* (tente, 2010). Akilah lived for many years in Boulder, Colorado, where she taught at the Naropa Institute's Jack Kerouac School of Disembodied Poetics. She also taught at Pratt Institute and The New School in New York City. She was a member of the Belladonna* feminist avant-garde collaborative and a graduate student in Philosophy, Art and Social Thought at the European Graduate School. At the time of her death, Akilah was living in Brooklyn and working on a book version of *The Putterer's Notebook* and her master's thesis, among other projects.

We would like to thank Barbieo Barros Gizzi for allowing us to include the original, complete version of her artwork entitled *The She Said Dialogues* on the cover of this edition. Barbieo created the image in 1999 in response to Akilah's book, and details of the image appeared on Akilah's original cover. We are also grateful to Eleni Sikelianos, Anne Waldman, Althea Abruscato, Teresa Hurst, Rachel Levitsky, Erica Hunt, Briar Essex and Juliette Palermo for important help along the way. Finally, we are deeply thankful to Tracie Morris for her beautiful foreword, and to Stephen Motika, Lindsey Boldt, HR Hegnauer, Jaye Elizabeth Elijah and the rest of the incredible Nightboat team for your patient and loving work on this book.

Akilah's work was always ahead of its time, and we are so thankful that these dialogues (or polylogues) with the self, with lovers, friends, family, time, god, memory, blackness as an eruptive force and so much more will continue to be heard in the world. We hope that communities everywhere will take this book and read it aloud together and share its gifts with one another to help us all continue to honor Akilah's important legacy.

Akilah, we miss you terribly. Your beautiful and challenging work continues to push us into the future through the force of its flesh memory.

With love,
Marcia Oliver, Laura Meyers and Rachel Zolf
August 2020

Nightboat Books

Nightboat Books, a nonprofit organization, seeks to develop audiences for writers whose work resists convention and transcends boundaries. We publish books rich with poignancy, intelligence, and risk. Please visit nightboat.org to learn about our titles and how you can support our future publications.

The following individuals have supported the publication of this book. We thank them for their generosity and commitment to the mission of Nightboat Books:

Kazim Ali
Anonymous
Jean C. Ballantyne
Photios Giovanis
Amanda Greenberger
Elizabeth Motika
Benjamin Taylor
Peter Waldor
Jerrie Whitfield & Richard Motika

In addition, this book has been made possible, in part, by grants from the New York City Department of Cultural Affairs in partnership with the City Council and the New York State Council on the Arts Literature Program.